This book belongs to

....

A Tall Tale and Other stories

How this collection works

This *Biff, Chip and Kipper* collection is one of a series of four books at **Read with Oxford Stage 4**. It contains four stories: *The New Year Race*, *Ship in Trouble*, *A Tall Tale* and *Roman Adventure*. These stories will help to broaden your child's wider reading experience. There are also fun activities to enjoy throughout the book.

How to use this book

Find a time to read with your child when they are not too tired and are happy to concentrate for about fifteen to twenty minutes. Reading with your child should be a shared and enjoyable experience. It is best to choose just one of the stories for each session.

For each story, there are tips for reading the story together. At the end of the story you will find four 'Talk about the story' questions. These will help your child to think about what they have read, and to relate the story to their own experiences. The questions are followed by a fun activity.

Enjoy sharing the stories!

Contents

OXFORD
UNIVERSITY PRESS

Authors and illustrators

The New Year Race written by Paul Shipton, illustrated by Alex Brychta

Ship in Trouble written by Roderick Hunt, illustrated by Alex Brychta

A Tall Tale written by Paul Shipton, illustrated by Nick Schon

Roman Adventure written by Roderick Hunt, illustrated by Alex Brychta

OXFORD
UNIVERSITY PRESS

Great Clarendon Street, Oxford, OX2 6DP, United Kingdom

Oxford University Press is a department of the University
of Oxford. It furthers the University's objective of excellence
in research, scholarship, and education by publishing
worldwide. Oxford is a registered trade mark of Oxford
University Press in the UK and in certain other countries

Roman Adventure first published in 1994
Ship in Trouble first published in 2007
The New Year Race and *A Tall Tale* first published in 2015
This Edition published in 2018

British Library Cataloguing in Publication Data
Data available

ISBN: 978-0-19-276430-0

10 9 8 7 6 5 4 3

Paper used in the production of this book is a natural, recyclable product
made from wood grown in sustainable forests. The manufacturing process
conforms to the environmental regulations of the country of origin.

Printed in China

Acknowledgements

Series Editor: Annemarie Young
Additional artwork by Stuart Trotter

Tips for reading *The New Year Race*

Children learn best when reading is relaxed and enjoyable.

- Talk about the title and the picture on page 6. Then read the speech bubble.

- Discuss what you think the story might be about.

- Share the story, encouraging your child to read as much of it as they can.

- Give lots of praise as your child reads, and help them when necessary.

- If your child gets stuck on a word that is decodable, encourage them to say the sounds and then blend them together to read the word. Read the whole sentence again. Focus on the meaning.

- If the word is not decodable, or is still too tricky, just read the word for them, re-read the sentence and move on.

- When you've finished reading the story, talk about it with your child, using the 'Talk about the stories' questions at the end. Then do the activity.

Children enjoy re-reading stories, and this helps to build their confidence.

Have fun!

For more activities, free eBooks and practical advice to help your child progress with reading visit **oxfordowl.co.uk**

The New Year Race

Which animal will win the race in Grandpa Chen's story?

Biff, Chip and Kipper went to have dinner with Lee's family.

"This is a special meal," said Lee. "It's New Year's Eve!"

"But New Year's Eve was weeks ago," said Biff.

"Chinese New Year is on a different day," said Grandpa Chen.

Lee and Lin were wearing red tops.

"It is a tradition to wear red for the New Year,"
said Lee.

"In our family we always have fish for dinner at Chinese New Year," said Mum.

"And we have these little dumplings!" said Lin.

At dinner, Chip asked Grandpa about Chinese
New Year.

"Each year is named after an animal. There are
twelve animals in all," said Grandpa.

"Tell them the story about the animals, Grandpa!"
cried Lin.

Grandpa began the story. "A long time ago in
China, there were lots of animals."

"There were tigers and dogs, monkeys and
horses," he said. "There were rabbits and snakes,
and even dragons."

"The Emperor wanted to name each year after a different animal," said Grandpa. "Which animal was going to be first?"

"The Emperor decided to hold a race for all the animals. The first year would be named after the winner."

"I think the tiger won the race," said Chip. "They're very fast."

"Rabbits are really quick, too," said Biff.

"I bet the dragon won!" said Kipper. "Dragons can fly! They would easily beat all the other animals!"

Lee just shook his head. "Nobody has picked the
right animal yet," he said.

"Tell them about the river, Grandpa," said Lin.

Grandpa went on. "The big day came. The animals had to race across a wide river."

"A river?" said Chip. "I wonder which of the animals was the best swimmer."

"Some snakes can swim well," said Biff.

"In fact, Ox was the strongest swimmer," said
Grandpa. "He was soon in the lead."

"Ox didn't know Rat and Cat had hopped onto his back," said Grandpa. "They planned to jump when Ox came close to the riverbank."

"I bet Cat won," said Biff. "Cats can jump much further than rats."

"Tell them, Grandpa," said Lin.

Just then there was a noise from outside. It was
a cat.

"Wait a moment," said Grandpa. "It is time for
my new year tradition."

Grandpa Chen put some fish on a plate. He opened the back door and called to the cat.

"What about the story?" asked Chip.
"Who won?"

"Rat did!" said Lee. "Cat slipped and fell
in the water!"

"By the time Cat finished the race, everybody
had left. Now there would be no Year of the Cat.
Cat was angry, especially with Rat."

"So why do you feed that cat?" Kipper asked
Grandpa.

"I was born in the Year of the Rat," said Grandpa.

"At the start of the New Year I like to feed this
cat to say sorry for the race!"

The cat walked away with its tail in the air.

"But look," said Grandpa. "Even now cats don't like rats!"

Talk about the story

What is the traditional colour for Chinese people to wear at New Year?

Which animal was in the lead at the beginning? Which one did you think would win?

Why did Grandpa Chen always feed the cat at the start of New Year?

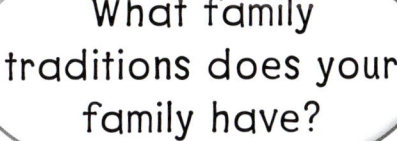

What family traditions does your family have?

Spot the difference

Spot five differences between the two pictures.

Tips for reading *Ship in Trouble*

Children learn best when reading is relaxed and enjoyable.

- Talk about the title and the picture on page 34. Then read the speech bubble.

- Discuss what you think the story might be about.

- Share the story, encouraging your child to read as much of it as they can.

- Give lots of praise as your child reads, and help them when necessary.

- If your child gets stuck on a word that is decodable, encourage them to say the sounds and then blend them together to read the word. Read the whole sentence again. Focus on the meaning.

- If the word is not decodable, or is still too tricky, just read the word for them, re-read the sentence and move on.

- When you've finished reading the story, talk about it with your child, using the 'Talk about the story' questions at the end. Then do the activity.

Children enjoy re-reading stories, and this helps to build their confidence.

Have fun!

For more activities, free eBooks and practical advice to help your child progress with reading visit **oxfordowl.co.uk**

Ship in Trouble

How did the children help rescue the crew of a ship in trouble?

Wilma's mum took the children to an adventure
playground. It was a new playground and it
looked exciting.

They all wanted a go on the zip wire. Chip went
first. It was hard to get on it, so Wilma's mum
helped him.

The zip wire went fast.

"Yee ha! This is scary," called Chip. "I love it."

Wilma was next, but she felt scared. Then the wind blew and it began to rain.

"It's too windy and it's raining," said Wilma. "I can't go."

"It's a bad storm," said Mum. "Let's go home.
We can come back another day."

So they all ran back to the car.

Wilf and Wilma went back to Biff and Chip's
house. They went to Biff's room to play.

"I hope we go back to the adventure playground,"
said Wilf. "I want a go on the zip wire."

Then the magic key began to glow.

The magic took the children back in time.
It took them to a cliff near the sea. A bad storm
was blowing.

Suddenly, there was a bang. A bright light lit
up the sky. Then a girl ran down the path. Behind
her was a man on crutches.

"Will you help us?" asked the girl. "The storm has blown a ship on to the rocks. The light in the sky was a call for help."

"We can't help," said Wilma. "You need to call the lifeboat."

"We can't," said the girl. "The lifeboat has gone to help another ship."

"My name is Jane," said the girl.

"I'm Jane's father," said the man. "I should be out with the lifeboat, but I've hurt my back."

"The ship is stuck on the rocks," said Jane.
"People are in danger. If you help us, we can
rescue them."

They ran to the lifeboat station. Jane loaded
things on to a donkey. She gave the children long
poles to carry.

They went back along the path. The waves
were crashing over the ship.

"This is a bad storm," said Wilf.

Jane told the children to lash two poles together.

"We must make sure they don't fall over,"
she said.

Jane's father had a special cannon. He shot a
line out over the water. The line flew through the
air and landed on the ship.

Jane tied a rope to the line. The people on the ship pulled it across. Then they tied the rope to the ship.

Jane's father put a pulley on the rope. The pulley had a ring tied to it.

"I get it," said Wilf. "The people sit in that funny-looking ring."

"Now we pull them in," said Jane.

"And I thought the zip wire was scary," said Wilma.

It was hard pulling the people across on the
pulley. The rope dipped in the middle and it
swung in the wind.

The last to come was the captain.

"I've lost my ship, but you've saved our lives,"
he said. "Thank you."

Jane looked at the children.

"Thank you for helping us," she said.

Then the key began to glow.

"I'm glad I wasn't on that ship," said Wilma.
"The zip wire at the playground won't seem
scary, now."

"Not even in a storm?" asked Wilf.

Talk about the story

What were the long poles used for?

How did the people from the boat get to shore?

How do you think the people from the boat felt?

What did you used to be scared of, but doesn't scare you anymore?

Crack the code

Here is another way to send a message. It is called Morse.

A •■	H ••••	O ■■■	V •••■
B ■•••	I ••	P •■■•	W •■■
C ■•■•	J •■■■	Q ■■•■	X ■••■
D ■••	K ■•■	R •■•	Y ■•■■
E •	L •■••	S •••	Z ■■••
F ••■•	M ■■	T ■	
G ■■•	N ■•	U ••■	

What message did the ship send?

••• •••• •• •■■•

••• •• ■• ■•■ •• ■• ■■•

••• • ■• ■••   •••• • •■•• •■■•

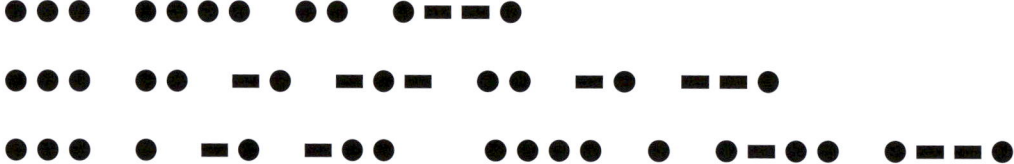

Tips for reading *A Tall Tale*

Children learn best when reading is relaxed and enjoyable.

- Talk about the title and the picture on page 62. Then read the speech bubble.

- Discuss what you think the story might be about.

- Share the story, encouraging your child to read as much of it as they can.

- Give lots of praise as your child reads, and help them when necessary.

- If your child gets stuck on a word that is decodable, encourage them to say the sounds and then blend them together to read the word. Read the whole sentence again. Focus on the meaning.

- If the word is not decodable, or is still too tricky, just read the word for them, re-read the sentence and move on.

- When you've finished reading the story, talk about it with your child, using the 'Talk about the story' questions at the end. Then do the activity.

Children enjoy re-reading stories, and this helps to build their confidence.

Have fun!

For more activities, free eBooks and practical advice to help your child progress with reading visit **oxfordowl.co.uk**

A Tall Tale

Uncle Max tells lots of tall tales. Will he enjoy a real adventure?

Uncle Max came for a visit. He brought presents for Biff, Chip and Kipper.

"These shells are from the other side of the world," he told them.

The children always loved to hear Uncle Max's
stories.

When they were ready for bed, he agreed to tell
them all about his latest adventures.

"Since I last saw you, I have been looking for adventure on the high seas," Uncle Max began.

"What happened?" asked Kipper. "What did you see? Was it dangerous?"

"Well, one time I went for a swim and was surrounded by huge stinging jellyfish," Uncle Max smiled. "Do you know what I did?"

"Not really," said Kipper.

"I had a brilliant idea!" said Uncle Max. "I pulled out a spoon and shouted, 'Yum, yum! Jelly for tea!' All the jellyfish swam off when they heard that!"

"Wow," said Biff. "But why did you have a spoon with you?"

"You never know when you might need a spoon," said Uncle Max.

"Another time a hungry shark wanted to eat me when I was diving for treasure," he continued. "So do you know what I did?"

"I'm not sure," said Kipper.

"Luckily, I had *another* brilliant idea," said Uncle
Max. "I scared that shark off with a sword."

"You had a *sword* with you?" asked Biff
in surprise.

"Not a real sword," said Uncle Max. "There was
a swordfish swimming past, so I used that!"

"Wow!" said Kipper.

"Is that possible?" asked Chip.

"You'd be surprised what can happen at sea,"
Uncle Max said. "Once I . . . "

He stopped and pointed at the light in the
corner. "Why is that key glowing?" he asked.

"It does that when it's taking us on an adventure,"
said Biff.

Uncle Max had no time to ask any more questions.
The magic took them all away.

It took them to a little boat in the middle of
the sea.

Uncle Max looked at the water all around them.

"What on earth's going on?" he asked.

The children told him all about the magic key.
"We go on lots of exciting adventures," said Biff.
"Just like you, Uncle Max," said Kipper.

A dark shape passed under the boat. It wasn't
just big. It was *enormous*.

"What was that?" asked Chip nervously.

"Um ... I'm not sure," said Uncle Max.

A huge whale's tail burst out of the water. It towered high above them.

"Come on, Uncle Max," said Kipper. "You must have a brilliant idea to escape!"

Before Uncle Max could answer, the enormous
tail slapped down on the water right next to the
boat. Splash!

It made a huge wave that carried the boat away.

The boat zoomed off, riding along the top of
the wave.

"This is just like one of your stories, Uncle Max!"
shouted Chip.

Uncle Max gripped the sides of the boat.

Another huge shape rose from the water in front
of them.

"An even *bigger* whale!" shouted Biff.

"Have you got a brilliant idea yet, Uncle Max?"
Kipper asked.

"Not just yet," said Uncle Max.

He didn't have time to say anything else. The whale's open mouth was like a huge cave and they were rushing towards it.

"Hold on tight!" shouted Biff.

The boat rushed into the whale's enormous mouth, along with seawater, seaweed and lots of silver fish. Everything went dark.

They stopped in a big, gloomy place.

"We must be in the whale's tummy!" said Biff.

Uncle Max looked around and shook his head.

"That's not possible," he said. "*Is it?*"

Kipper gave Uncle Max a hopeful look.

"How about now?" he asked. "Any brilliant
ideas for how to get out?"

"No!" groaned Uncle Max. He looked soggy
and miserable.

For a long time the only noise was the gurgling
of the whale's tummy.

Suddenly Uncle Max jumped up. "Wait! I *have*
got an idea," he shouted, "and it's a *brilliant* one!"

He began to rock the boat from side to side.

"Join in!" he told the children. "If we do it enough, I'm sure it will make the whale burp!"

There was a rumbling noise all around.

"I think it's working!" said Kipper.

Biff gripped the sides of the boat. "We'd better
hold on tight again," she said.

Just then Biff spotted a bright light. The magic
key was glowing, at last.

"Don't worry," she said. "There's a much easier
way out of here!"

The next moment they all were safely back in
Biff's bedroom.

Uncle Max blinked. He looked around the room,
rubbed his eyes and blinked again. He scratched
his head.

"Sorry, children," he said. "I think I fell asleep for a moment. I had the *strangest* dream!"

Biff slipped the magic key into her pocket.

Uncle Max noticed something.

"How on earth did this tiny bit of seaweed get on my sleeve?" he asked.

The children glanced at each other and grinned.

Uncle Max held the seaweed between his
fingers.

"Actually, this reminds me of the time I had
a tickling competition with a giant octopus,"
he said.

"Wow! That sounds amazing," said Biff. "What did you do?"

"Luckily I had a brilliant idea," said Uncle Max. "Can you guess what?"

"Not really," said Kipper happily.

"Well," said Uncle Max, "earlier that day I had made friends with an electric eel ... "

The children snuggled down to enjoy one more tall tale before bedtime.

Talk about the story

What was Uncle Max's brilliant idea to scare off the shark?

How did they all end up in the whale's tummy?

What did you think about Uncle Max's idea for them to escape?

Do you like to tell tall tales?

Tell a tall tale

Play this game with some friends.

1 The first person thinks of something they will take in Uncle Max's boat beginning with A.

In Uncle Max's boat I will take an **a**pple.

2 The next person thinks of something beginning with B.

3 The game keeps going. When someone gets something wrong, they are out.

In Uncle Max's boat I will take an **a**pple and a **b**alloon.

Tips for reading *Roman Adventure*

Children learn best when reading is relaxed and enjoyable.

- Talk about the title and the picture on page 98. Then read the speech bubble.

- Discuss what you think the story might be about.

- Share the story, encouraging your child to read as much of it as they can.

- Give lots of praise as your child reads, and help them when necessary.

- If your child gets stuck on a word that is decodable, encourage them to say the sounds and then blend them together to read the word. Read the whole sentence again. Focus on the meaning.

- If the word is not decodable, or is still too tricky, just read the word for them, re-read the sentence and move on.

- When you've finished reading the story, talk about it with your child, using the 'Talk about the story' questions at the end. Then do the activity.

Children enjoy re-reading stories, and this helps to build their confidence.

Have fun!

For more activities, free eBooks and practical advice to help your child progress with reading visit **oxfordowl.co.uk**

Roman Adventure

What happens when the children go on a Roman adventure?

Biff and Chip were doing a project on the Romans.
The project was for Mrs May. Biff made a chariot
and Chip drew a picture.

Mum and Dad looked at the project.

"The Romans are interesting," said Biff. Chip showed Mum his picture. It was a picture of a Roman chariot. The chariot was pulled by four horses.

Biff showed Dad the model.

"The Romans had chariot races," said Biff. "The races were dangerous. A chariot was so heavy, it needed four horses to pull it."

Mum and Dad played a joke on Biff and Chip.

They dressed up as Romans.

"It's time for supper," called Dad.

Kipper had some pizza and Mum had
some grapes.

"This is a Roman supper," said Mum.

"Romans didn't have pizzas," laughed Biff.

"How do you know?" asked Mum.

Biff and Chip went to Biff's room. Biff wanted
to take the chariot to school, but she still had
to paint it. Chip was good at painting, so he
helped Biff.

Suddenly, the magic key began to glow.

The magic took Biff and Chip on a new adventure.

"Oh no!" said Biff. "I'm still painting the model chariot."

The magic took the children back to Roman times. It took them to Rome. Biff and Chip saw a girl. She was playing in the street.

The girl looked at Biff's model. "It's a good model," she said, "but it doesn't look quite right." "We've never seen a real chariot," said Biff.

The Roman girl was called Diana. She had a brother called Mark. He was a chariot driver. Mark looked at Biff's model chariot.

"I can show you a real chariot," he said.

Mark opened some big doors. Inside was a real chariot. It was like Biff's model, but it was very big.

"Wow!" said Biff.

Mark let Biff go on the chariot. Biff pretended she was a chariot driver. She pretended she was in a race.

"I wish I could be a chariot driver," said Biff.

Mark laughed at Biff.

"You have to be strong to race chariots," he
said. "I'm in a race today. Come and watch it."

Everyone was hungry, so Diana took the
children home.

"We can have some bread," she said. "My father
is a baker. He makes the best bread in Rome."

Everyone looked at the bread, but something
was wrong. The bread didn't look right. It was
flat. It didn't look like bread at all.

Diana's father made some more bread. He baked it in the oven, but it was flat, too.

"This is bad," said Diana's father. "Nobody will buy bread like this."

Chip looked at the flat bread. He had a good idea.

"We can make pizzas," he said.

"What are pizzas?" asked Diana. "We don't
know what pizzas are."

Chip told Diana's mother how to make pizzas.
Everyone helped. Diana's mother cooked the pizzas
in the big oven.

The pizzas looked good.

"I hope you like them," said Chip.

"Everyone likes pizzas," said Biff.

"They smell good," said Diana's mother.

The pizzas tasted good too. Diana's father
was pleased.

"Now we can sell them," he said. "We can sell
lots and lots. What a good job the bread was flat."

They went outside to sell the pizzas, but there was nobody in the street. There was nobody to buy the pizzas.

"Where is everyone?" asked Biff. Everyone had gone to the chariot races.

Diana's father was upset. He looked at
the pizzas.

"All that work for nothing," he said. "How
can we sell pizzas when everyone is at the
chariot races?"

Diana had an idea. She put some pizzas in
a basket.

"Come on," she called. "If everyone is at the
chariot races, we can sell the pizzas there."

They took the pizzas to the chariot races.

"Come and buy a pizza," called Diana.

But nobody bought the pizzas. Everyone was looking at the races.

The children saw Mark, so they gave him one of the pizzas.

"These pizzas are good," said Mark.

Biff looked at the chariot and she had a good idea.

The children had a banner. It was about the
pizzas. Mark put it on his chariot. The people
laughed when they saw the banner.

"Why has Mark put a banner on his chariot?"
people asked. "And what are pizzas?"

The race began and everyone cheered when
Mark came first.

The people ran to buy the pizzas.

"These pizzas are good," they said. "What a good idea to put a banner on the chariot."

Just then, some soldiers grabbed the family and the children.

"You must stop selling pizzas," they said. "The Emperor wants to see you. Come with us."

The Emperor was angry.

"This has got to stop," he said. "Who put this banner on the chariot? And what are pizzas?"

"Would you like to try one?" asked Diana.

"They taste good," said the Emperor. "You can deliver some to the palace. But I don't want banners on the chariots, so take your banner away."

Just then, the magic key glowed.

Chip looked at the little banner. He put it on
Biff's chariot.

"The Emperor didn't like banners on chariots,"
he said. "I wonder what Mrs May will think."

Talk about the story

How did Mark's chariot look different from Biff's model?

Why was there no one in the street?

Why did Diana's father look worried when he was told the Emperor wanted to see him?

What do you like to cook?

Obstacle race

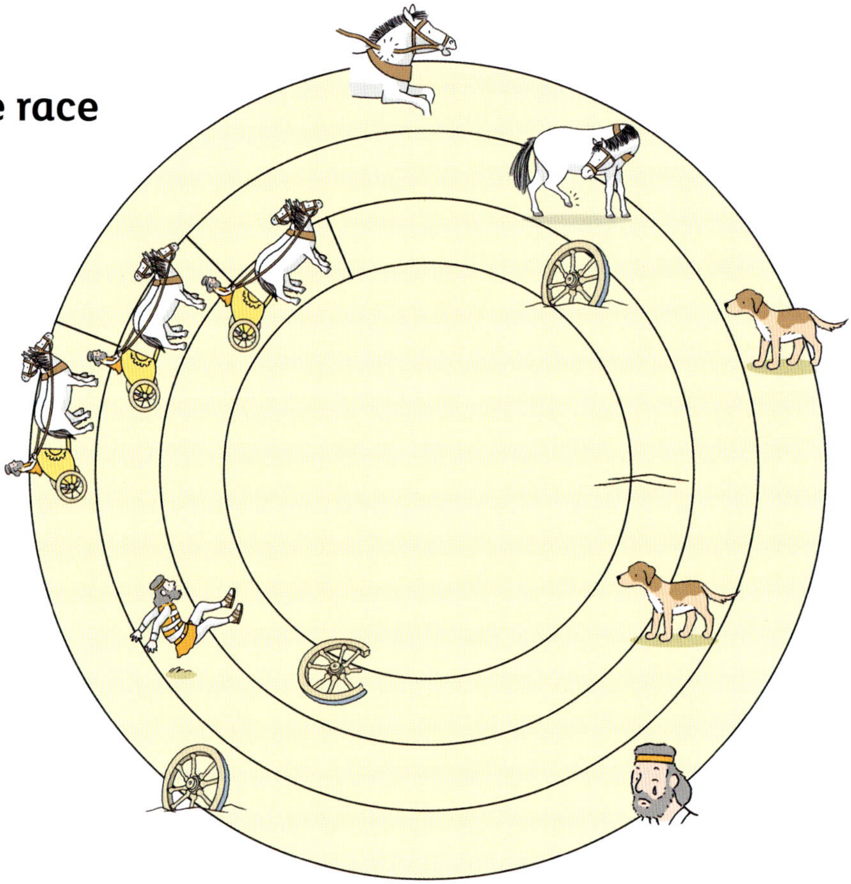

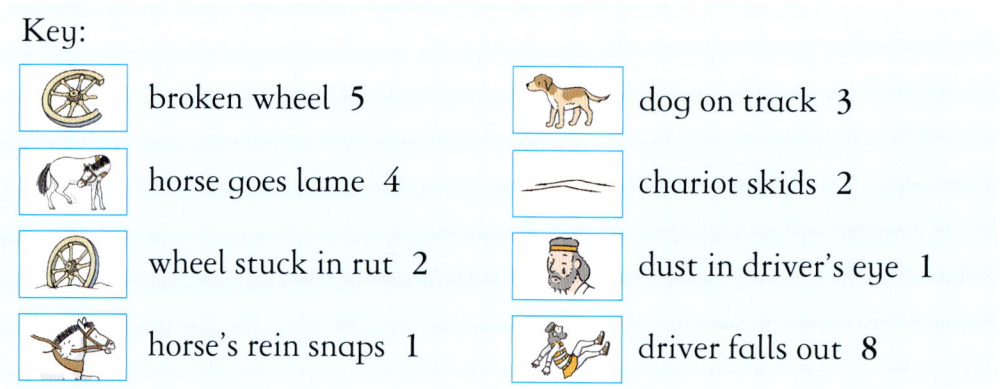

Which chariot wins the race? Look at the obstacles in each race lane, check the key and add up the scores for each chariot. The chariot with the lowest score wins.

Key:

broken wheel 5		dog on track 3
horse goes lame 4		chariot skids 2
wheel stuck in rut 2		dust in driver's eye 1
horse's rein snaps 1		driver falls out 8

Remembering the stories together

Encourage your child to remember and retell the stories in this book. You could ask questions like these:

- Who are the characters in the story?
- What happens at the beginning of the story?

- What happens next?
- How does the story end?
- What was your favourite part of the story? Why?

Story prompts

When talking to your child about the stories, you could use these more detailed reminders to help them remember the exact sequence of events. Turn the statements below into questions, so that your child can give you the answers. For example, *What are the children celebrating?*
What do they learn about Chinese New Year? And so on …

The New Year Race

- The children are having a special Chinese New Year dinner.
- They learn about Chinese new year traditions and the twelve animals that represent each year.

- Grandpa Chen tells them the story of how the animals were selected. There was a competition.
- The rat wins the race, but he makes the cat fall and come last, so there's no year named after the cat.

Ship in Trouble

- The children go to a new playground, but it starts to rain, so they go home.
- The magic key takes them back in time where a ship has run aground.
- The children go to get things to help from the lifeboat station.

- They attach a rope and pulley to the boat to pull the people in along the rope.

A Tall Tale

- Uncle Max is telling bedtime stories when they all get taken on a magic adventure.

- The magic key takes them to a small boat in the middle of the sea.

- An enormous whale appears and the children expect Uncle Max to have an excellent idea to save them, just like in his stories.

- Eventually Uncle Max has an idea to make the whale burp so that they get pushed out of its stomach.

- Thankfully it's not needed, as the magic key glows and takes them home.

- Uncle Max thinks it was all just a dream and carries on with his bedtime stories.

Roman Adventure

- Biff is making a Roman chariot for a school project when the magic key takes them on an adventure to the Roman times.

- A girl called Diana invites them to watch a real chariot race.

- Everyone is hungry before the race, so they go to eat some bread at Diana's father's bakery, but the bread is flat.

- The children suggest making pizzas instead, which nobody has heard of.

- They take the pizzas to the chariot race to sell.

- The Emperor tells them to stop selling pizzas, but once he tastes one, he decides they're ok after all.

You could now encourage your child to create a 'story map' of each story, drawing and colouring all the key parts of them. This will help them identify the main elements of the stories and learn to create their own stories.

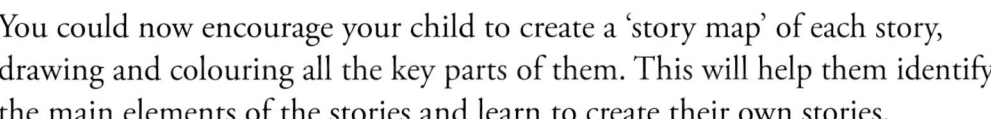